# Your Life Matters!

By Julia Myles

# TABLE OF CONTENTS

# Author's Note:

TO GOD BE THE GLORY!!

THIS IS A LABOR OF LOVE FOR ALL WHO READ THE
PAGES OF THIS BOOK!

*There is a rhythm and flow that works for Julia – it's a
part of the balance and the syncopation of the
inward heartbeat.*

*That balance is projected outwardly throughout my
life.*

*"Freedom begins inside you."*

Love & Blessings!

– J. Myles

**Personalize this book**

**Name:**

**Date:**

**Location of purchase:**

**We create our own memories each day.**
**Make yours memorable!**

# What's Your Story?

## Why this book?

People write for many reasons: pleasure, employment, attention from others, because they're inspired, and many other motivators.

I am writing this book as a labor of LOVE. I want to write my story so that you, the reader, will be inspired to write your own story.

As a child, I remember our pastor, Pastor Odom, would get up on Sunday night before Testimony Service and say, "Everyone has a story to tell."

I am borrowing that phrase because I believe everyone does have a story to tell.

My story begins with a vision:

In my mind's eye, I stood at the pew during a church service last year, standing, listening, and observing all that was happening around me. I saw a book cover with the words **"BOOK of Julia V1."** I remember the background color on the pages was white, and that it was a series.

I must write as the Holy Spirit inspires me.

As you have guessed by now, I am a believer. I believe each of us was created for a purpose and each of us has a destiny. I also believe that my actions and steps are ordered by God.

As a natural person having a supernatural experience in this earth realm, your steps are ordered by God. You may not have the awareness of that statement now, but one day I believe you will.

Here is the revelation you might not see or accept: Yes, even as an unsaved or backslidden person, your steps are ordered by God. I call him God; you may call him by another title.

I believe God allows every step you and I take. His inspired word is over you, in you, and through you.

## How does this book apply to you?

As you read this book, you may notice a few recurring themes or repeated words of wisdom. Let me explain. As a teacher and a student, I realize that we learn by repetition. In my life, the lessons I remember most are those I had to repeat over and over.

For example, when I was younger, I thought I was smarter than the average bear, as most kids do. I always thought I could get away with things because I would be quiet and sneaky – like knowing when my dad was asleep and taking a few pieces of candy from his "secret stash," or putting my hand over his face while he was laying on the couch to make sure he was really asleep. I did it a few times, until I got caught.

I remember that spanking very well, but I still tried it again!

That's the life we have. Sometimes we repeat and repeat until we get it right, or get caught doing wrong.

## Life is composed of many experiences

It has been said that experience is the best teacher. I will share my personal experiences throughout this book. Some were good experiences, some were painful, some were happy, and some were life-changing.

You will read about my childhood experiences – my family dynamic, why I believe in God, (the good, the bad, and the not-so-good experiences!)

I want to be as transparent as possible because there will be some life lessons in each experience that will help you as you begin to review your life.

You may be thinking, "What do I have in common with this woman?" or, "What do I have in common with this African American woman?"

We are all human.

We are all living.

We all need air, water, food, and some form of shelter.

We all desire to live our best life.

We all believe that we are important, and that we matter.

We all love to be loved.

We all bleed red blood.

The list could go on and on, but believe I know one thing for sure – we are more alike than we are different, the same way as David and Jonathan "became one in spirit," we are, "united in the same joints." And that is why we are more alike and the main reason why we are all connected. This also explains how we can be edified by the common connections.

The following scriptures further explain my point:

"And it came to pass, when he had made an end of speaking unto Saul, that the soul of Jonathan was knit to the soul of David, and Jonathan loved him as himself."
– 1 Samuel 18:1

"From whom the whole body fitly joined together and compacted by that which every joint supplieth, according to the effectual working in the measure of every part, maketh increase of the body unto the edifying of itself in love."
– Ephesians 4:16

## My life lesson: this writing experience

I'll end this chapter with a short recent experience. I wrote original volume of this series last December as I was taking time to reflect on what had occurred in 2016. As a member of the John Maxwell team, I have an awesome group of mentors. On occasion, we are mentored as a group by Maxwell. He speaks about daily reflection in many of his books.

As I was reflecting last year, I dictated the first five chapters of this book, then transcribed the first two chapters into a self-published book.

I was so excited about what I had accomplished that I took the book with me to a women's conference in February at which I was a vendor as well as an attendee.

A few weeks after the conference, I got a phone call from two young ladies who had purchased my book. They are great, young, professional women and wanted to give me their feedback.

I will never forget that phone call. Have you ever been embarrassed and angry at the same time?

They were very honest with me and I listened. We talked about the cover and the contents and they gave me their honest feedback. Some of their comments included:

"If this book was in the store – I wouldn't even pick it up."

"There is nothing on this cover that catches my eye."

"You are a member of the John Maxwell team. This book is nowhere near their level of publication."

"You need to get a professional photo shoot."

I thanked them for their feedback, wrote down some notes, and hung up the phone.

I was embarrassed and angry, partly because I am in a leadership position and partly because they were right. Really, my ego was bruised. I am human. It happens.

It took several months of "planned procrastination" – if you are not familiar with the term, that's when you self-sabotage by filling up your schedule with other things to avoid the main thing you should be doing – and a series of events and divine intervention to get me to this revised book.

So, I thank them for their love and their feedback. I thank you for purchasing and reading this book.

## **Thought-provoking questions:**

What is one life-changing memory from your childhood?

_____

_____

_____

_____

Have you thought about writing your story?

_____

_____

_____

_____

What is the title of your book?

_____

_____

_____

_____

# Connections

"We are all connected, whether we choose to
believe it or not!"
– J. Myles

"I am the vine, you are the branches. Whoever
abides in me, and I in him, he it is that bears much
fruit, for apart from me you can do nothing."
– John 15:5

## Natural connections

Have you considered the way things are
interconnected? I think about the simple things –
the links in a chain, the fingers connected to our
hands, the toes connected to our feet, our arms

and legs connected to our bodies.

I love trees. I have always loved trees, possibly because I grew up in the desert and other than a few cacti and other transplanted trees, trees were not the norm.

Look at the tree from top to bottom – no, let's look at the tree from the bottom up. If we look below the surface of the dirt, the roots of the tree are there. As we move up the trunk of the tree, we see how the tree bark covers the tree, the branches are connected to the trunk, and the leaves are all part of the branches.

I have two very old oak trees in my backyard. They have huge limbs, and what fascinates me the most about the trees are their roots. The trees are more than 15 years old and the roots are so thick they are always popping out from under the ground.

It's amazing that the sturdiness of a tree is due to the strength of the root system below it. We have lived through tornadoes, windstorms, rainstorms, and multiple hurricane watches, and those two trees remain strong, as if resting in the storms.

These natural connections can also have their symbolic and spiritual meanings, as the tree of life in the garden of Eden was Jesus.

The LORD God planted a garden toward the east, in Eden; and there He placed the man whom He had formed. And out of the ground the LORD God caused to grow every tree that is pleasing to the sight and good for food; the tree of life also in the midst of the garden, and the tree of the knowledge of good and evil.
– Genesis 2:8-9

He who has an ear, let him hear what the Spirit says to the churches. To him who overcomes, I will grant to eat of the tree of life, which is in the Paradise of God.
– Revelation 2:7

We have natural connections. We have trees that provide us with oxygen that we need to breathe to live. We (believers) have Jesus, the Son of God, who gives us life just like the tree of life.

In this case, we need to question ourselves. What are we connected to? What are we attracted to the most? Do we have strong roots? Are you rooted and grounded in your belief system?

If we are lacking strong roots, we won't be able to endure the challenges we face in life, or evolve. On the other hand, roots of bitterness can lead to the complete destruction of the tree. A healthy root system will determine the spiritual or natural fruit in our lives.

"Since he doesn't have any root, he lasts only a little while. When suffering or persecution comes along because of the word, he immediately falls from faith."
– Matthew 13:21

## Personal connections

There are so many connections in our lives. We have friends, relatives, acquaintances, in-laws, outlaws, neighbors, coworkers, etc. As you read God's book, there are connections from the Old Testament and New Testament, familial connections, generational lineage, friends, relatives, etc. You have the same type of connections in your life. People who have your DNA, both in the natural and in the spirit.

As you think about the current personal connections in your life, consider the following questions:

- Who are you connected to?
- Are all your connections profitable for growth?
- Do they provide comic relief to you?
- Are they leeches?
- Are they edifying for the spiritual, natural, physical, and mental part of you?
- Are your connections rusty?
- Are they outdated?

- Is it time to refresh, renew, update, or reset all the connections in your life?
- Do your connections bring glory and honor to God?
- Be honest with yourself – are your connections fruitful, or are they fruitless?
- Do they bring you pain or pleasure?
- Are your connections bringing you closer to your destiny, or pushing you farther away?
- Are your connections edifying?
- If not, do you ask yourself why?

Think about each of the questions and then listen intently for your response. The first real response. Don't accept the preprogrammed auto response – **I don't know** – that will immediately come up in your brain. We normally accept the most comfortable answer that our brain or intellect comes up with. As part of this chapter, I am asking you to consider what you think and how you feel about the current people connections in your life.

I have gone through this exercise several times over the past two years. I remember distinctly how I felt when I realized how many of my "connections" were no longer as relevant to me as they were in the past. I am a people person, so my mindset had to shift to really accept the fact that many of my previous connections were no longer relevant to who I am right now. I know that might sound harsh to some of you. I don't mean that I disregarded them as people; I respect and love them the same way or even more. However, I had to come to the realization that they were in a place that I was quickly moving away from, both in the natural and in the spirit.

"So when they saw Him, they were amazed; and His mother said to Him, 'Son, why have You done thus to us? Look, Your father and I have sought You anxiously.' And He said to them, 'Why did you seek Me? Did you not know that I must be about My Father's business?'
– Luke 2:48-49

Even Jesus had similar experiences with personal connections. He respected and loved his mother, father, and brothers; however, He was moving away from them to complete the heavenly father's purpose. This example reflects how changing personal connections pushes people to their destiny.

## Letting go of your past connections to save your future

As we grow and evolve we sometimes look back, in awe of where we came from. Many of us came from humble beginnings. I often tell people, "We were poor, but really never knew it!"

I remember how small my parents' house seemed when I returned from living out of town for several years. It's amazing how big it seemed when I was growing up. In actuality, it was a two-bedroom, one-and-one-half-bath house with an add-on room in the back. When my sister and I had to go back and prepare the house to be sold, I walked through it and thought, "How did all eight of us – six kids and two parents – fit in this house?"

The neighborhood, and specifically that house, hadn't changed, but I had. My friends and acquaintances were no longer there. They had moved on. Most of us had grown up and left the city and the state, moving on to bigger and better things.

Trees, as I talked about earlier, reach upward even if they are crooked, or even planted sideways. This reminds us to always reach upward, as trees do naturally. Some trees also produce fruit, and although they may produce less fruit due to bad weather or climate changes, they still produce – they are not paralyzed by the circumstances. Some trees – most trees – produce more when they are pruned or cut back.

You may wonder why I keep referring to the trees. I see a similarity between people and trees. When trees (people) go to the next season, "they succeed in everything they do –- like trees, we bear fruit in season" (Psalms 1:3).

But enough about trees; let's keep going with the story.

I realized my mindset had to change for me to move away and not return to the past. That is also true of some of my past connections. Have you ever gone back and heard this statement from friends or family: "Boy, you have really changed! You are definitely not the person we knew!"

When I hear that statement now, that is a great statement. To you, it might be an insult. I am happy about it because I have changed and evolved. The only thing constant about our lives is change. However, many people don't want to change. They fear change and anything associated with it because change is unfamiliar and requires more work. Also, we are not in control because the purpose of change is to mold our character, as God is constantly molding us to His character of love and courage. This is the reason why in Exodus 3:14, "God said to Moses, I am that I am," because God is His character.

When I attend high school and sometimes family reunions, I am always asked, "Is that you, Julia?" I expect to get that question, so I am used to it. I am no longer the shy, quiet, introverted person I was. That is a good thing!

Growth, personal and natural requires us to change and evolve. The fear comes in when we are faced with opposition from friends and others, and from our inner self (that comfort zone) that longs for the past. Sometimes, the fear of the future is more comfortable than the fear of the past. The ability to really see the difference of where we were and who we are and understand that life is really about change will help you move past the fear of losing your connections and the fear of making new connections.

We grow and get renewed day by day. Our personal and natural connections can be the instruments used to mold our character in order for us to evolve.

"Therefore we do not lose heart. Though outwardly we are wasting away, yet inwardly we are being renewed day by day. For our light and momentary troubles are achieving for us an eternal glory that far outweighs them all."
– 2 Corinthians 4:16-17

## Let's think about it

Take some time to **go deeper within and ask God to show you** the closest **five** people you associate with. Write their names:

1. _____

2. _____

3. _____

4. _____

5. _____

Take a good look back over the past 365 days and assess your relationships with each one.

Now the heartfelt hard part: Who are you willing to let go?

You may not have any connections to let go of. That's wonderful. Carry on.

However, if you do have to let some of your current connections go to move forward, to the next place, the higher level, or on to the next season – realize everyone can't or won't be with you.

"To everything there is a season, and a time to
every purpose under the heaven."
– Ecclesiastes 3:1

## You must be willing to move forward anyway

This doesn't mean you don't love them or don't
appreciate them. It means you have chosen to
take this part of your journey without some of
them.

You have a right to make a choice! Give yourself
permission to succeed.

Give yourself permission to move and walk by
faith. Give yourself permission to trust God and
trust the process.

By trusting the process, you will have to cross over
to the next season, the next place, and/or level,
just as Mark 4:35 talks about "passing over." We
cannot be afraid to fulfill God's purpose for our
lives.

"And the same day, when the even was come, he
saith unto them, Let us pass over unto the other
side."
– Mark 4:35

It is time for you to move over to the other side.
Time for you to move to the next level.

**Your notes on Connections:**

_____

_____

_____

_____

_____

_____

_____

**Your action steps to improve the Connections in your life:**

_____

_____

_____

_____

_____

_____

_____

# Release From Fear!

"For God has not given you the spirit of fear!"
– 2 Timothy 1:7

My journey with fear began many years ago. As a young child, some of my earliest memories include me hiding under the kitchen table, running to hide in a closet, or being afraid of something about to happen.

I grew up in a home with my mom and dad and five siblings. My dad was a military man who commanded and demanded respect and order.

If things weren't done right, there were consequences.

The consequences would include my father's drinking. This was not an every-weekend experience, but if things occurred during the week that he was upset about – whether business related or home related, it would manifest into his drunken anger.

The main target of his anger was my Mom, and as we grew up and tried to defend her we became part of the process.

I was the youngest girl in my family. I have two younger brothers and three older siblings. My father had an alcohol addiction. Actually, he was what some call a functional, or weekend, alcoholic. My father and mother's relationship was long lasting – they were married about 55 years before my dad passed.

When my dad drank, he would come home, wake everyone up and make all of his complaints known to us and, I'm sure, to our neighbors. There were several occasions when he would physically abuse my mom. As my brothers got older, they would step in to protect my mom, which turned into another night of fighting, yelling, and screaming.

My favorite vantage point during those times was from under the kitchen table. I would "hide" with my fingers in my ears to soften the angry voices, crying, and screaming.

Sometimes, he would settle down and fall asleep. Sometimes, the police would be called. I was crippled by fear during those moments. As I got older, I would walk outside with my mom to be with her when she waited for the police to come, or stand with her as she spoke with concerned friends or neighbors.

I am sure some of my readers can relate to that or a similar situation in one way or another.

As a result of witnessing the abuse, I grew up afraid of my dad. He represented the main authority figure in my life at that time.

That fear of my earthly father shaped the way I viewed my heavenly father. I knew God loved me, but I was always fearful of what He would do if He was angry at me.

**The fear factor: Types of fear**

I'm happy and grateful to report that mindset about fear has changed.

Many people are paralyzed by different types of Fear:

> Fear of the unknown
> Fear of failure
> Fear of success
> Fear of acceptance
> Fear of heights
> Fear of flying
> Fear of people
> Fear of insects
> Fear of spiders
> Fear of fod
> Fear of not measuring up
> Fear of meeting new people

The list can go on and on. I am sure you could give me at least 10 fears you have right now, or have experienced in your life.

Within the fear of people, we can include the fear of man. Fear also creates anxiety in the process, but there is always someone available to help us release those fears.

> "Fear of man will prove to be a snare, but whoever trusts in the Lord is kept safe."
> – Proverbs 29:25

> "When anxiety was great within me, your consolation brought me joy."
> – Psalms 94:19

## What is fear?

Fear is defined, by Webster as an unpleasant emotion caused by the belief that someone or something is dangerous, likely to cause pain, or a threat. Or, to be afraid of (someone or something) as likely to be dangerous, painful, or threatening.

A good friend of mine defines fear as False Evidence Appearing Real!

As a trainer, encourager, coach, and friend, I want to understand why clients, students, and friends have fears, and find a way – within my level of assistance – to help people overcome them.

"So do not fear, for I am with you; do not be dismayed, for I am your God. I will strengthen you and help you; I will uphold you with my righteous right hand."
– Isaiah 41:10

## How to release fear

"I sought the Lord, and He answered me and delivered me from all my fears."
– Psalm 34:4

This is a timeless issue. I am sure there are many answers and thoughts on the topic of how to release fear. My use of the word "release" vs. "lose" is intentional. My mentor reminded me that when you "lose" something, there is a possibility of finding it again. When you release something, there is intention of letting it go. You do it on purpose with intention.

I quickly adopted that phrase, and I am releasing things, people, attitudes, etc. all the time.

My research turned up several ways to conquer/release the fears:

**Identify the fears**. Take the time to recognize and identify your fears. This may be as simple as writing out a list and reviewing each fear. Or, it can be more involved, talking with someone you trust, or a trained counselor or professional. Either way, the first person to identify your fears is you.

**Talk about the fears**. Once you have identified your fears, the next step is to talk about them. I believe that the things we keep secret, or hidden, can kill us physically, emotionally, and spiritually. As stated in the previous step, there is always someone you can talk to about your fears.

**Confront the fears.** Depending on the type of fear you are facing, you may be able to face them head on. I am not advocating facing them alone: I would strongly recommend a counselor or trained professional to help you face the fear. What worked for me – counseling and prayer – may not work for you. However, there is a method of confronting the fear that will help you overcome it.

**Use exercise, meditation, prayer**. Many of the fears we face cause unnecessary stress. I am a huge proponent of routine exercise, daily meditation, and prayer. I have friends who add yoga to their fear-release program, which has helped them to overcome fear.

## There is hope

If you are reading this chapter and saying, "Yeah, but you don't know how I feel," or, "You haven't been through the same experiences I have," that may be true. But I have successfully overcome fear in my life and I would like to share a bit of my journey with you.

It all begins in your mind. "As a man thinketh ... so is he."
– James Allen)

"For as he thinketh in his heart, so is he..."
– Proverbs 23:7

Fear is a feeling based on emotion, just like any other emotion that we all possess. All fears are not bad. Fear can be a great motivator – I'm sure you've heard the slogan, "Do it afraid!!"

Fear can be turned around in an instant, such as people who are in a dangerous situation, or trying to rescue a loved one, or even skydiving.

Remember the show Fear Factor? Contestants would go on the show and face their fears to win money. I always wondered how much money it would take for me to eat live worms. They don't have enough!

We all have fears. In some cases, we create ways to avoid them. In other cases, we create ways to ignore them – but eventually, at one point or another, we will have to deal with our fears.

One fear I overcame is the fear of what people thought of me. I called it the fear of public opinion. There came a time in my life during which so much was going wrong, and I didn't have any control over what was or wasn't happening in my life, that I decided to give up. This was a process – it didn't happen overnight.

I remember praying and asking for guidance. I was so embarrassed by the mess in my life. I wanted to end it all. But in reality, I was more fearful of dying, and I didn't want my kids to be motherless. I was so full of anguish and pride. I didn't realize I was depressed. I was laying in my apartment and not doing anything useful. My kids were with their dad for the weekend. One of my friends stopped by to check on me. Good thing she didn't call first, I probably would not have answered the phone.

She could tell I was not well. She asked me how I was doing. I responded, "I don't know, I'm just lying here on the couch." She said, "Julia – this is not like you." I responded, "I know, but I couldn't deal with the internal pain at the time." We chatted a while and she left, but before she left she looked at me and said, "You know, this is not the end of the world. You are stronger than this." I just looked at her, thanked her, and told her goodbye.

I didn't feel stronger. I was afraid of what was happening, and I didn't want to deal with it.

That was the last time I saw her; she passed away the next week and I never had the opportunity to tell her thank you.

Needless to say that moment was a wake-up call for me.

I did what I could to face my fear. I swallowed my pride and asked for help. I had counseling and prayer and I made the effort to move beyond what I was afraid of.

One day this saying came to my mind: "It doesn't matter what people think – They don't have a heaven or hell to put you in."

I don't know where I heard it – but I adopted it and I asked God to help me be free of public opinion. I have never looked back.

That was more than 25 years ago. I have faced many fears since that time, and I am sure I will face more as I continue my life journey. The point is, everyone has or has had fears.

Yes, everyone, whether they admit it or not. I learned to face and overcome fear, and you will, too. The fears will always be there. They'll be waiting for your weakest moments, constantly reminding you of your past. But when you're willing to face the fear, you'll see that all the things you are fearful of are meaningless.

The release-of-fear process begins with you, and there are also a few verses that may help you if your method of assistance is similar to mine: meditation on the Word of God, consulting with trained counselors, and prayer.

"Cast your burden upon the Lord and He will sustain you; He will never allow the righteous to be shaken."
– Psalms 55:22

"casting all your anxiety on Him, because He cares for you."
– 1 Peter 5:7

"The Lord has taken away His judgments against you, He has cleared away your enemies. The King of Israel, the Lord, is in your midst; You will fear disaster no more."
– Zephaniah 3:15

## FEAR

## @JCTM – December 21, 2008

We Look at the unknown and are afraid

We Look at the past and we are afraid

Someone will find out the tiny "secrets"

We are hiding

We look at ourselves

Do we measure up?

Am I acceptable?

Will I fit in?

We look at others

With quiet envy

Why can't I look like that, talk like that, dress like that? If we would accept who we are

How we were created in God's Image

With His character, vision, love, peace, and joy!

We have no fear

We are fearless!!

F.E.A.R. = **F**alse

          **E**vidence

          **A**ppearing

          **R**eal

               Think about it.

## Your notes on fear:

_____

_____

_____

_____

_____

_____

_____

_____

_____

_____

_____

_____

_____

_____

_____

_____

_____

_____

_____

_____

_____

_____

_____

_____

# Healing

"The Lord will keep you free from every disease.
He will not inflict on you the horrible diseases you
knew in Egypt."
– Deuteronomy 7:15

No matter how deep the issue is and no matter
how long you have struggled with it, the possibility
exists for you to become absolutely free, whole,
and healed.

## Repair yourself

What the world needs now, more than ever
before, is healing. Healing in our homes, our

schools, our cities, all across the nations of the world. We need healing.

The basic definition of healing is the process of becoming whole. Healing is less about fixing yourself than it is a practice of letting go. It helps you release blocks — physical, emotional, and mental blocks and behaviors that keep you limited in your potential and true health.

There are many types of healing and many beliefs about healing. If you look up the topic, you will find information on medical healing, self-healing, alternative healing, integrative (combined) healing, and more.

In this chapter, I want to discuss emotional, physical, and spiritual healing, and how they are integral to our lives.

Let me begin with my personal experiences.

I grew up in a home with more prayer and anointing oil than trips to the doctor. Throughout my childhood – as most children do – I had the typical childhood illnesses – chicken pox, measles, sore throats, colds, etc. When we were sick, the first thing my mother would do was anoint us with oil and then lay hands on us and pray. If my dad was home and noticed we were sick, his first move was to call my mom.

I remember one event when I was 5 or 6 years old

– I went into the backyard of the house and attempted to climb the Wire Fence. I was curious about what was in the Alley behind the house. I thought I could make it over the fence and explore. I assume the fence was about 5 feet high, it had crisscrossed wires at the top that were sharp to the touch. I didn't realize that until I was almost to the top. With one leg in a hole for balance, I swung the other leg over and a prong got stuck in my leg. I didn't scream – because I didn't want to get into trouble – but it was painful.

So there I was, by myself, stuck on the fence in the backyard. My mom came outside and saw me on the fence. As she got closer, she saw the blood on the fence and me there barely holding on. She didn't say a word. She pulled my leg off the fence and brought me back inside.

She was silent as she cleaned up the blood and put the oil on my leg and my forehead. I never went to the doctor or received any medication. Only prayer.

It's funny the things you remember. There was another time when I was about 9 or 10. My dad had the barbecue pit fired up in the backyard to smoke the meat for his restaurants. If you grew up like I did, and your father was the sole proprietor of a family business, guess where the employees came from! In this business, everyone in our house had to help him when he prepared the meat.

One night, I was bringing him the meat tray and was near the door of the smoke pit where the fire was burning. Anxious and in a hurry to get back inside because it was dark outside and cold, I wasn't paying attention. When I got too close to the barbecue pit, I didn't see that the door was open a little bit – but I sure felt it!!

I burned the front of my thighs on both legs. I still have traces of the scars. Once again, praise God, no hospital trip, just prayer.

Some of you may wince at these childhood memories or relate them to similar experiences. All I can say is that I knew if I was sick, my mom would pray for me and I would get well.

Physical healings are also tied to spiritual or emotional healing. As previously discussed, we are all connected. This is why a person dealing with depression can seem physically drained. Sometimes the physical healing does not come through, because the emotional healing has to come first.

There were other occasions in my life when I needed more than just physical healing. I needed spiritual and emotional healing.

Spiritual healing is when the human spirit becomes damaged and sick from the effects of sin in our lives.

The Cambridge English Dictionary defines spiritual healing as the "activity of making a person healthy without using medicines or other physical methods, sometimes as part of a religious ceremony: Spiritual healing has an ancient pedigree, with much evidence of success. Alternative and traditional therapies."

Spiritual healing can also be viewed as a physical healing.

For example, I have heard that a person was praying for a young lady and strange things were happening. This young lady had skeletal system issues, but nobody knew anything about them, as the skeletal problems were hidden from view.

In this case, the prayer of spiritual healing led to a physical healing. The young lady's body was completely restored and she could finally stand up straight without pain.

During that prayer, everybody was listening to the "cracking" sound of her bones and were completely astonished. There were no indications of pain in the cracking process, and nobody knew what was happening in the spiritual realm or the physical realm.

Everyone was shocked that her body started to be completely straightened. They knew this was the work of God. No one physically touched her after praying for her because they knew that God was doing something that could not be seen physically.

There are many cases of physical and spiritual healings in the word of God.

This skeletal-system healing example is actually compatible to what Psalm 34:20 says, "For the Lord protects the bones of the righteous; not one of them is broken."

Apparently, this young lady was born with those skeletal-system problems, but God decided to restore her miraculously because she was a profound believer in our lord and savior Jesus Christ. Her spiritual healing led to a physical healing because:

- She released her past.
- She released her fears.
- And she loved the Lord with all her heart.

She had a process in which she had to first receive spiritual healing and then receive complete physical restoration.

"He sent out his word and healed them, and delivered them from their destruction."
– Psalms 107:20

This young lady did not fear going to her next season. She could now do many things that she could not do before that healing. This is also showing us that we have to be healed and remain in that healing in order to go to our next season.

## What is a soul tie?

Spiritual healing involves the healing of the soul, spirit and physical.

Wikipedia defines "soul" as follows: "In many religious, philosophical, and mythological traditions, there is a belief in the incorporeal essence of a living being called the soul."

The word "soul" in the Bible is a translation of the Hebrew word *ne'phesh* and the Greek word *psy·khe'*. The Hebrew word literally means "a creature that breathes," and the Greek word means "a living being." The soul, then, is the entire creature, not something inside that survives the death of the body.

While we are all spiritual beings inside a human body, there are times when our spirit (soul) is damaged, hurt, and/or broken. The term spiritual healing is a very broad term, and can mean many different things across different cultures. For the purposes of this chapter, I will briefly discuss the common types of spiritual healing.

From a biblical perspective, there is no actual reference to the words "soul tie." However, it is understandable how the term came about. The term was derived from the words "united" and "become one flesh." These words imply a joining together of a man and woman which creates a connection – the two souls becoming one flesh.

You see this idea repeated in traditional wedding vows. This idea is repeated in the following scripture:

"For this reason a man will leave his father and mother and be united to his wife, and the two will become one flesh."
– Genesis 2:24

A soul tie is described as a linkage in the soul realm between two people. This connection links their souls together, which has the possibility to develop positive or negative results.

Examples of positive (healthy) soul ties are formed in family relationships, marital relationships, friendships, etc. These ties can create fulfilling and loving bonds between their members.

Soul ties are not exclusive to relationships between people, they can also involve spoken words. Other examples of positive soul ties can include wedding vows, commitments, and promises. Positive soul ties are very important, and following them creates a healthy environment.

The word of God also talks about the importance of keeping vows in Numbers 30:2: "If a man vows a vow to the Lord, or swears an oath to bind himself by a pledge, he shall not break his word. He shall do according to all that proceeds out of his mouth."

Positive speech (affirmations) can be exemplified as follows:

- "My life is moving in the direction of the positive words I speak!"
- "Amazing things happen to me every day."
- "I do not fear the future. I am courageous."
- "My life is a miracle."
- "I carry peace in my heart."
- "Every day and in every way – I am getting better and better."

A negative (unhealthy) soul tie may be formed through abusive (verbal, physical, and emotional) sexual relationships. Examples of how negative soul ties are formed include – rape, physical abuse, molestations, incest, adultery, and fornication (sexual relationships outside of marriage).

Vows, commitments, and promises can also have a negative approach. An example of a vow with a negative approach is the following:

- Negative confessions – "I will never get over what you did to me."
- Inner vows – "I will always be broke," or, "I will always have this struggle."
- Word curses – "You are a failure," or, "You will end up like your father."

This is why we have to be careful how we speak to ourselves and to others. James 5:12 says, "But above all, my brothers, do not swear, either by heaven or by earth or by any other oath, but let your 'yes' be yes and your 'no' be no, so that you may not fall under condemnation." Proverbs 12:18 also tells us that, "the words of the reckless pierce like swords, but the tongue of the wise brings healing."

It is amazing to know that "a wise tongue brings healing." I understand that sometimes it is difficult to have a wise tongue. But if we are careful with our "speech," we can accomplish many things.

A soul tie can also be a "yoke." In history, a yoke is mostly used in a symbolic manner as in slavery to a foreign king. A yoke is also used to force two individuals to move together. In this case we have to ask ourselves the following:

- What are we yoked or tied to?
- Can we move together peacefully or in violence?

Sometimes when you are constantly feeling weak or oppressed, you may have a negative soul tie or yoke that has to be undone.

Your very own words could be keeping you trapped to a bad soul tie, which explains why you feel like something is pulling on you, preventing you from fully going forward.

Sometimes we become our own words and, "we shall eat the fruit of those words," just as described in Proverbs 18:21. It's very similar to "we reap what we sow." Words have authority and, "Death and life are in the power of the tongue, and they that love it shall eat the fruit thereof."

We can also use the example of trees that I talked about in the beginning of this book to reflect that the growth of the tree, the natural connection, depends on the seed, which can even be through a simple word.

Words can also bring health, as Proverbs 16:24 teaches us that, "Gracious words are like a honeycomb, sweetness to the soul and health to the body."

## Release from soul ties

Prayer is an essential step to gain a release from soul ties.

Giving God the first position in your life is the key. You must be willing to submit to Him and admit that you need help.

Pray daily for your heart to heal from the wounds of the past and always remember to, "guard your heart, for everything you do flows from it" (Proverbs 4:23).

Ask God to give you strength to move past the hurt and pain from the broken relationships.

The Bible reminds us to, "pray without ceasing." Matthew 7:7 also states to, "ask and it shall be given to you."

After my first divorce, I sought prayer for release of the soul tie I had with my first husband. I know from experience how the role of prayer affects this area.

## Study God's word daily

The words we speak are of the Spirit and they are life. Words have the power to create, and we are the creators. The power of death and life is in our mouth. Words are carriers. The words we speak can affect change to our life, health, physical, and emotional well-being.

Have you heard the saying, "You are what you eat?" That saying also holds true for what we read and speak.

Negative soul ties keep you in bondage and fear. Especially the fear of failure.

The links or ties you have from past sexual encounters are all stacked up inside of you – and your relationships will continue to fail until you ask for help to remove the past from your mind, body, and spirit.

Bible reading and studying are great resources to find encouragement, strength, and healing. This will give you great inspiration and practical advice for moving forward.

In terms of something being tied, Wolters Kluwer, author of the *Indian Journal of Psychiatry*, said that the word of God and prayer are considered a positive soul tie and that, "Prayer has been reported to improve outcomes in humans and to have retrospective healing effects."

Other researchers and passages in the Bible draw the same conclusions:

"More things are wrought by prayer than this world dreams of."
– Alfred, Lord Tennyson

"Faith can move mountains."
– Matthew 21:21

## Let them go!

Isaiah 10:27 says, "And it shall come to pass in that day, that his burden shall be taken away from off thy shoulder, and his yoke from off thy neck, and the yoke shall be destroyed because of the anointing."

I grew up in a family that kept everything. My parents were part of that generation that held onto things longer than necessary. You probably have a drawer of items or box of items in your closet from your past relationships – pictures, cards, letters, and gifts. All constant reminders of something that no longer exists. You look at them and long for something that doesn't exist anymore. You want to move on to a new relationship while holding on to the previous ones.

You have become double-minded. Double-mindedness leads you to either failure or instability. "A double-minded man is unstable in all his ways."
– James 1:8

You have to let them go. I know he told you that you were the only one for him – or she said you were the only man she would ever love. Those words and memories are keeping your heart locked up. The thoughts are holding you in bondage. Forgive yourself – forgive them and let them go.

You might be like me, grown in the Christian faith and a current believer. Or perhaps you would like to start praying like I do because you have no other resources or alternatives right now. The most important step is to just focus on the Lord Jesus and repeat the following prayer to release soul ties and/or yokes:

"In the name of Jesus Christ, I renounce and release _____ (name of the soul tie or name of a person or habit) and I release myself and my descendants from all emotional, physical, and spiritual yokes, captivity, slavery, and soul ties because 'all yokes shall be destroyed because of the anointing.' And I order a full release of all negative ties that do not let me pass to the next season in the name of our lord Jesus Christ. I thank you, Jesus, for the freedom you have established for me. Amen."

## My life lesson – Spiritual healing

My spiritual healing began when I realized I needed to be free from sin. I grew up in a very religious environment, so I always had some type of sin consciousness. I really didn't understand it fully as a child, but that was the way we were taught.

As I got older, I recognized a lot of disparity between the way I was taught and the way other people lived – I think we all have experienced this at one point or another in our lives. We question it as children, but we really live it when we get older.

I made a decision when I was 17 to really, truly live for Christ. I wanted to be all in. I had made confessions of salvation earlier, but this time was different.

So my life moved forward, based on the God I was taught about as a child and the God I learned about as an adult.

There was an instance in my life where I realized I had relied upon my mother for everything spiritual in my entire life. I was in Germany, married and pregnant with my first child. I never really realized how much my mother's prayers meant to me until I had to learn to pray for myself.

I became very aware that my spiritual life, my personal relationship with God, had to get deeper or I wasn't going to make it.

I made the decision to reach out to God for his help. I also made the decision that I would follow the teachings in the Bible for the rest of my life.

That worked perfectly when things were going well. However, when things went downhill after about 10 years of marriage – I mean really bad – my faith was shaken. How could this happen to me? I was clueless. I had this preconceived idea that everyone should treat me the way I treated them and that people in the church should behave a certain way – especially my husband, who was a preacher.

I had to learn this lesson the hard way: We are all human and we are subject to Fail.

So my spiritual healing after the divorce began with forgiveness. Forgiveness of him, her and, most importantly, forgiveness of myself. That was a huge step.

Forgiveness is more about releasing others in order for you to be released than it is about going through the motions. When you live in unforgiveness, you not only hold others hostage, you hold yourself hostage. And you keep yourself in bondage.

For example, I heard of an elderly woman who did not forgive her ex-husband for his infidelity. This caused great struggle and division every time there was a family reunion for the holidays. The person who has had to deal with this aftermath is their son, who he cannot together in the same room with his father and mother. The son wants to have family gatherings, but the ex-wife does not want to socialize with the father's new wife, creating a complete separation and awkwardness of what the son once called family gatherings.

This example reflects how you can keep yourself in bondage and make others forcefully join you in those bondages.

I took many steps forward – and backward – in this process. Eventually, after doing my internal work, I made progress.

So I thought.

## Moving forward and then backward

Life has a way of bringing you into focus. Fast-forward 17 years after the first divorce, and my second husband – the man who I thought would be my last husband – announced he didn't want to be married anymore.

There I was again. Really, Jesus??? I guess for some of us, the healing journey takes longer than for others. We are the ones who keep ourselves in a desert for a long period of time. My emotional healing process began when I realized during the second marriage that I felt I loved him more than he loved me. I haven't shared this information before – even though I have been very transparent.

My second marriage was very secure financially. We were living the dream. My children were grown up and out of the house. My husband and I had successful careers and we did lots of things together. But there was always this feeling in the back of my mind that something was just not right.

I lived in denial for a very long time. I just went along to get along.

I was accepting, tolerant, and very forgiving. But I was not happy inside. There were many times when I felt so alone, and I couldn't tell anyone but

God. I wanted our marriage to work but I had to face the fact that it was over.

Here we go again, with the divorce lawyer and drama, drama, drama ... and then it was over.

I was faced with the pain, agony, and the embarrassment of being a saved woman, a pastor, and divorced twice.

Emotional healing can be described as the healing of the soul, to a point at which a person no longer has an emotional reaction to either the sins that they have committed or the sins that have been committed against them.

Christian author and motivational speaker Joyce Meyer states:

"If you want to receive emotional healing, one of the first steps you must take is to face the truth. You can't be set free while living in denial. You can't pretend that certain negative things didn't happen to you."

## Breaking the cycles

There comes a time in each of our lives where we realize what we are doing, and see that how we're living is not working. Have you ever felt like the hamster in a wheel, going around and around but getting nowhere? Has your life been a series of doing the same thing repeatedly, with different people, and getting the same results?

The people of God were in the same repeated cycle. This entailed that they did not get to see the promised land, the next season. They did not accept change and did not evolve.

However, two individuals entered into the promised land. Joshua, which in Hebrew means Jehovah Saved, also another name for Jesus, and Caleb, which in Hebrew means wholehearted or faithful. We can think about it this way: The faithful and wholehearted walked with Jesus to enter the promised land. They accomplished the goal of going to the next season. We should do the same.

## Same cycle, different players

I repeated the cycle of divorce for the last time. I decreed that word over myself: "I will do things differently the next time and I will receive better results." I learned from this experience. I know you have family and friends who have been in similar situations.

My emotional healing – loving myself enough to be honest with myself, learning to love me again, learning to work through the emotional damage, and overcoming the unrealistic expectations of myself and my old mindsets – has been part of this second phase of my healing.

This is a period of discovery and rediscovery of who I am. Sometimes we get stuck in our story, so much so that we can not move forward. I realized that in order for things to be different I had to change, inside and out.

I began to evaluate all the parts of my life; friendships, relationships, how I respond, what I think and why I think the way I do. I asked myself the hard questions. Questions like, "What do you really want? What will you do differently? How do you feel about yourself? What makes your heart sing? When is the last time you really enjoyed your own company?"

I determined that I would love myself enough to ask for help in the areas I couldn't figure out by myself. I began to become my own empowerment counselor.

Acknowledging I had a part to play in the demise of the relationship was key. Sometimes we are guilty of accepting things the way they are, or going along to get along. We push our emotions aside in order to avoid conflict. I was very guilty of that and had to decide to speak up for me. I was capable of speaking up and fighting for everyone else, and now it was my turn to speak up for myself.

I wish I could say it's all over, but I can't. I wish I could tell you it was easy, but I won't. What I can tell you is what I know for sure: I am better than I was four years ago, and I am grateful each day for who I am.

I am in this journey for life. My life – Your Life Matters!

## Your notes on healing:

_____

_____

_____

_____

_____

_____

_____

_____

_____

_____

_____

_____

_____

_____

_____

_____

_____

_____

_____

_____

_____

_____

_____

_____

_____

_____

_____

_____

_____

_____

_____

_____

_____

_____

_____

_____

_____

_____

_____

_____

_____

_____

_____

_____

_____

# Conflicted

"Elijah approached all the people and said – How
long will you hesitate between two opinions? If the
Lord is God Follow Him, but if Baal, follow him. But
the people did not answer him."
– 1 Kings 18:21

I am reminded of a phone conversation I had with
an old friend. When I left Texas, I did not keep up
with the majority of the people I associated with.
This was intentional with some, and others, we
just lost touch. When I received the phone, one of
the first questions they asked was, "Julia, what
happened?"

Without missing a beat, I blurted out, "Change
happened."

The change conversation began in my mind. When I began this journey in 2010, my mind conversation can best be described as, I was conflicted! A part of me wanted to be who God had ordained me to be. At that time that was the only thing I could relate to – pastoring, church, and being a minister of the gospel was all I had in me. Or, that's all I knew up until that moment.

Was it fulfilling? Yes and no.

Was it restricting? Yes and no.

The conversation in my mind was the same as the title in this chapter: Conflicted.

## How do you make a God-led decision?

Some life skills are taught, others learned. Decision making is a life skill that each of us need.

Every day, we have the opportunity to make decisions. Nothing in our life just happens. When I told my friend that change happened, it was an easy way for me not to answer the question, and also a way for me to avoid reality.

Sometimes, we love to live in a fantasy where nothing is ever our fault, everyone else has problems, and all things happen to everyone else and not to us.

But even the word of God states that there are brothers and sisters all over the world going through the same things we are going through:

"Whom resist steadfast in the faith, knowing that the same afflictions are accomplished in your brethren that are in the world."
– 1 Peter 5:9

There are also times when we want everything to be someone else's fault.

Having the ability to make sound decisions and following through with the decisions you make is a life skill. Successful people will tell you that they make a decision and follow through.

Godly decision-making makes you take heed of the following questions:

- Can this decision jeopardize my integrity?
  Proverbs 10:9 says, "He who walks in integrity walks securely, but he who perverts his ways will be found out."
- What are the outcomes for my decision?
  Proverbs 14:15 says, "The naive believes everything, but the prudent man considers his steps."
- Do I have all the facts?
  Proverbs 18:17 says, "The first to plead his case seems right, until another comes and examines him."

You can research godly decision-making; there are many books and ideas to help you figure out what to do. I'm all about keeping things simple, concise, and also practical.

I'll share a bit of my process and continue my story.

First, I ask God for guidance. This can be as simple as a prayer, or it can be a series of prayers and fasting for a few days or weeks.

Second, I review the word of God to make sure that what I am doing is in line with God's plan for me and the vision God has given me.

Third, I write a simple outline of what I want to do, the timeline for accomplishing it, and what resources (people, funding, etc.) will be required to include a begin and end date.

Fourth, I begin to execute the plan.

Fifth, I evaluate the progress after 30 days, revise where needed and continue.

## Back to my story

> "For I know the plans I have for you, declares the Lord, plans to prosper you and not to harm you, plans to give you hope and a future."
> – Jeremiah 29:11

I made some bold steps in 2010, deciding to obey God and follow the path that I knew that was set before me. In August of 2011, Healing Waters Ministries International Fellowship, Inc. began. This ministry is still in existence today.

The original mandate for Healing Waters was to provide a platform for others, and for the first couple of years, I did that. The first three years, I held annual conferences and invited speakers. As the ministry continued, it was still not fulfilling the true purpose of Healing Waters. The true purpose was being revealed to me as I continued to work and learn what it means to be in ministry.

The purpose of ministry is to put a demand on us to empty ourselves so that Jesus can come out. This is actually the high calling of God. Our ministry – just like Jesus emptied Himself to reflect the Father.

Also, we are not here to be right, we are here to be conformed to be right. That is when change happens.

I accepted a temporary assignment as assistant pastor for a local ministry and in three years, I learned a lot of lessons. I put the ministry on hold to focus on that assignment. I am grateful for it, because it further solidified the fact that I was not designed to be a full-time, behind-the-pulpit pastor. That is not in my spiritual DNA.

Not saying that I couldn't do it – I could – but it was not the assignment for me. I would not be happy and I had to face that fact to move on. I realized that I am built for a different vision in ministry.

## Change happens again

Once my pastoral assignment ended, I realized that there was an opportunity for me to expand. I had a desire to do more and become more. I remember praying, and after praying – I spoke this declaration out loud, and I know it was inspired by the Holy Spirit – I wrote it in my journal:

"I want to be mentored by millionaires."

At that time, I had read a lot of books but not anything in the genre related to personal growth, self-help, or anything not related to religion, or the word of God, or to following that formula.

I never wanted to be labeled as a "religious" person. I always believed that the God I serve is bigger than what my mind or someone else's mind could put it in and I never ever want to put God in a box.

So, I was searching on Facebook and I saw an advertisement for the John Maxwell team. I clicked the ad, and that's how my next journey began. I became a member of the John Maxwell team in 2015.

One of the membership benefits is mentorship, and guess what? I am currently "mentored by millionaires."

For example, in Joseph's story – he was the one in the Bible who was sold into slavery by his brothers – we can say that he was mentored by millionaires. These millionaires were the high-standing officials in Egypt at that time. He ended up being the right hand of Pharaoh, and Pharaoh reflects a high-economic-standing official.

## What's next?

That's a question people ask me from time to time. "What's next? How do you move forward? How did you deal with all the changes in your life?"

I understand. My life is moving in the direction of the words I speak. I say this all the time, both as a declaration and as a reminder.

The words we speak can change our minds and our brains. It has been proven that our words can affect our nervous system. Studies have proven that thoughts, and what we speak, can either improve or negatively affect our fitness, strength, and many other things.

We can shape our destiny by the words we speak, the thoughts we think, and the actions we take – daily.

"I will persist until I succeed."

Persistent action = consistent results

In Greek, the word "confession" means "to say the same as." I believe in persistent action, therefore, I speak consistent results before they happen. Afterwards, those consistent results become reality. "We shall eat the fruit of our words," as previously stated. So this reflects that "confession" brings us to experience.

In order to achieve the "next" on my life, I must be consistent, persistent, and clear on who I am and what the vision is.

The Comfort zone in your mind will always say, "What if?" What if YOU fail? What if you don't? What if this happens? It all has to do with our mindset, and my mindset has shifted.

I don't have the same mind in many ways that I had when I first moved to Alabama in 2003. I am not that same woman! I am not that same person. Because my mind and my thoughts have changed, evolved, and transformed.

I have seen and experienced things that I never imagined I would, both in the natural and in the spirit, and in the physical and emotional realms as well. But all of that taken together has brought me to this point in my journey.

The main point is metamorphosis will occur in your life. You will change – you will broaden and deepen who you are. Don't accept the or idea that where you are right now is where you will always be. If you keep breathing and keep on living, as the old people used to say, you will change.

Change is inevitable, whether you take charge, move forward and help manage it, or sit back and let it happen to you.

When Jesus opened the eyes of the blind, God gave a blind man a spiritual vision before the physical vision took place.

"And he looked up, and said, I see men as trees, walking. After that he put his hands again upon his eyes, and made him look up, and he was restored, and saw every man clearly."

– Mark 8: 24-25

Remember how we also talked about trees in the beginning of this book?

This Bible verse states that the spiritual vision of seeing men as trees is a reality. People are like trees and Jesus is the tree of life, as discussed in previous chapters. People are trees that have seeds, which are the fruits of their mouth (what they speak). This blind man was open to change and was restored.

Either way, change will happen.

## Your notes on Conflicted:

_____

_____

_____

_____

_____

_____

_____

_____

_____

_____

_____

_____

_____

_____

_____

_____

_____

_____

_____

_____

_____

_____

_____

_____

# The Importance of Prayer

"My prayer life is the foundation of my spiritual growth. It is the wind beneath my Wings."
– J. MYLES

Confess your faults one to another, and pray one for another, that you may be healed. The effectual fervent prayer of a righteous man avails much.
– James 5:16

Prayer is a part of my daily spiritual practice. Many people have experienced the power of prayer. Others have heard of prayer, or experienced their pastors, priests, rabbis, mothers, fathers, uncles, aunts, or grandparents praying for them.

I do also encounter people who have never prayed, or don't know how to pray, and some who have never prayed out loud. This chapter will help you, the reader, understand what prayer is and provide some basic information about prayer. I do not assume that everyone reading this book prays.

## What is prayer?

Prayer is a form of communication, A conversation between you and God. To me, it is as simple as a conversation with a friend.

The Web Dictionary states that prayer is, "A solemn request for help or expression of thanks addressed to God or an object of worship.

A religious service, especially a regular one, at which people gather to pray together.

An earnest hope or wish.

Wikipedia states, "Prayer is an invocation or act that seeks to activate a rapport with an object of worship through deliberate communication. Prayer can be a form of religious practice, may be either individual or communal and take place in public or in private."

There are many types of prayer and just as many reasons to pray. There are times in our lives when nothing but prayer makes sense . I know this to be true. When you have encountered sickness, pain, hurt, disappointments, and you believe in God or your higher power, you have uttered a prayer.

There are so many current events, tragedies, national/international disasters, and mass shootings that bring many to pause and ask, "Does God hear us when we pray?

For example, an individual from the Bible was dying, but prayed and moaned fervently until God replied with healing:

"Go, and say to Hezekiah, Thus saith the Lord, the God of David thy father, I have heard thy prayer, I have seen thy tears: behold, I will add unto thy days fifteen years."
– Isaiah 38:5

Can you imagine that? Hezekiah's prayer had positive results and God increased his years of life.

Some of us were taught to pray or say grace over our daily meals, especially at Thanksgiving or on Sundays. Others have seen prayers during television programs, or have read about prayer or meditation. Every religion has some form of prayer practice or meditation. The practice of prayer is universal.

As a Christian, prayer has played an integral part in my life. I love to pray.

## Why I love to pray

I enjoy the freedom of expression that I have in prayer. I love the time I spend with God. The time I spend in prayer is like a great adventure, being built each day. I can come to God boldly, loving the time I spend. My prayer times are great.

There are those who say I am called to pray. I would counter that statement with the scripture that says, "... man ought always to pray, and not to faint" (Luke 18:1).

My prayers have increased in strength and consistency over the years. There was a time when I didn't know how or what to say when I prayed. I learned to overcome this by consistent praying and also by listening to others pray.

I learned by example. Praying in a group setting where everyone was given an opportunity to pray aloud helped me to become comfortable praying.

Practice makes perfect.

Recently, someone reminded me of a quote:

> "When the student is ready, the teacher shows up."

I pray without ceasing. Does that mean I am praying 24/7 – 365? No. However, I am in a mindset and posture – ready to pray always. My life is a life of prayer. As I stated in the previous paragraph, at the basic level, prayer is a conversation between you and God. It is communication.

Sometimes I think we make it harder than it needs to be. Many times, we are afraid of saying something wrong, when in reality, there is nothing you can say to God in prayer that would catch God off-guard.

He is always available to us and ready to hear what we have to say.

## Learning by doing

I am not making light of what prayer is, I simply want to express the simplicity and remove some of the mystique. Sometimes I think we make things harder than they need to be.

My earliest memories are of my mother praying with us, at meals before we went to school, and before we went to bed. My mom, Winnelle, was a very beautiful woman, both inside and out. She was my cousins' favorite aunt. She had lovely, wavy black hair and was a very proper woman. She was a petite woman in the natural – but a very strong woman in the Spirit.

I remember that she was always kind and generous to everyone in word and in deed.

We were taught to pray and about the importance of prayer. My childhood may be similar to yours if you were brought up in some form of religion. I know this is not always true. There are people don't think about prayer, who believe they have made it this far in life without it. My mother did not work outside the home. Her specialty was prayer, fasting, and training the six of us in the way that we should go.

Mom was always an example of a praying woman. People would call her on the phone for prayer. She would make sure to pray for them as they called. She belonged to several prayer groups and would regularly go to hospitals and nursing homes to pray for those in need. Of course, I would have the wonderful experience of accompanying her when I was not at school. Trust me, at the time I didn't think it was a wonderful experience. However, as I have gotten older, I cherish those memories of spending time with my mother and watching her minister to others. In a sense, she was training me for my future.

## Prayer changes you

As you can imagine, in my eyes, Mom was always connected to God. She had deep experiences with prayer and fasting. She was a 40-day-and-beyond faster. I now know the secret to her success.

Let me share the secret with you: When you pray, prayer changes you first, then it changes circumstances and how you view and relate to people around you.

There is a place in God, a place in prayer where the stillness of peace and the exhilaration of joy overflows constantly.

The bond of prayer is very important to every person, especially believers. I am a product of the prayer legacy: My mother's family includes many preachers, pastors, teachers, educators, professionals, etc. The common thread that links us together is prayer.

It has been said that, "prayer is the key that unlocks the door." I don't know who said it first, but I have heard that saying all my life.

As I studied the life of Jesus, I found that Jesus went from one place of prayer to the next, and performed signs, wonders, and miracles in between.

I love that. I live that. I do love that my time with God is precious.

## Healing benefits of prayer

Healing of our physical bodies is a great benefit of prayer. Many religions across the world believe in the power of prayer for healing. In the United

States and in other countries, prayer remains an important source of strength for people who are sick.

Some studies have found that, a persons involvement in religious activity increases their mental and physical health while improving their social confidence.

The religious activity referred to above includes prayer and Bible reading. Another study showed that prayer is helpful in lowering anxiety and helping people to cope.

I have experienced the healing benefit of prayer. I know for a fact I was healed from the effects of a blood clot and high blood pressure through the power of prayer. My life is a constant testament to the power of prayer.

In the *Indian Journal of Psychiatry*, several scientific experiments were conducted concerning prayer that led to positive results, vs. the absence of prayer, which led to negative outcomes.

In his book, Wolters found that, "women who had been prayed for had nearly twice as high a pregnancy rate as those who had not been prayed for (fifty percent versus twenty six percent)."

This was just one statement, however, the statement motivates me more to pray even though I already love praying. Can you imagine the benefits and positive results increasing more than fifty percent? I consider this an outcome of prayer.

## My life is prayer

Please don't assume this has always been my spiritual practice. I didn't just arrive at this life of prayer, it has evolved throughout my life. It is the best tool in my spiritual tool bag. Prayer is my best weapon in my strategic weaponry arsenal. Prayer takes me places that I never thought possible.

I love and live the agreement where two or three come together, Jesus is in the midst. The connected prayer of agreement is exponential. "One can chase 1,000, two can chase 10,000." You know the multiplication of agreement prayer in the scriptures. If you don't, look it up. Memorize it.

As I have continued in prayer, God reveals and has revealed so much to me. I learned about the gifts of the Holy Spirit, and being filled with the Holy Spirit.

I learned to embrace the value of praying in the spirit and praying with an understanding. I was filled with the Holy Spirit by the laying on of hands in a prayer meeting.

I will never forget the prayer warriors and teachers who labored with me and prayed for me throughout my life: My mother, Terry Evangelist A. Walker, and Mother Adams.

All three of these ladies have passed away, however, the life lessons they taught me, and others are priceless. They taught by example.

I desired all my life to live by example, and yes it has come to pass: I can now be that example for the next generations, for as far as I can reach in this season in my life.

There is even a new season globally that we all should consider. There is a new season even in medicine and science. Even the Washington Post states that, "prayer is the most common complement to mainstream medicine, far outpacing acupuncture, herbs, vitamins, and other alternative remedies."

There are more recent studies that certify and prove the reason why I prefer prayer rather than alternative medicine.

Studies about prayer were published in 2000 in the *Annals of Internal Medicine*. This publication indicates that, "Thirteen studies showed positive results, meanwhile only one showed a negative result. This increases the benefits of prayer to almost ninety percent in this study."

"Prayer takes you to places no man has been." I understand Paul the Apostle as he talks about prayer. I know and have experienced dreams and visions. I understand and operate in spiritual authority and dominion, all because of prayer. Prayer is foundational.

Prayer and my connection to God keep me from falling. "Now unto Him who is able to keep you from falling. To the one who presents me before the father, before the presence of his glory with exceeding joy, to the only wise God" (Jude 1:24)

God is the who!!

You gain wisdom through prayer.

Jesus presents you to God joyfully when you pray. When you pray, God gets all the glory; all the majesty belongs to Him. He gave it and he gives you the keys — wisdom, knowledge, understanding, peace, favor, abundance, truth, patience, long-suffering, healing, and wholeness. Dominion! I'm standing in Him . My relationship with God is greatly enhanced, solidified, and strengthened – connected – through prayer.

As I stated earlier, I love to pray! There's a place in God, a hidden place where you can't be touched or moved. You are covered, hidden. I know this is a recurring theme in my life and I repeat this key to others all the time.

I had a vision of God's hand as I prayed. Imagine a hand the size of the largest mountain you have seen. I saw the tiny speck in the center of the huge hand, and as the magnification increased, I could see the speck in His hand was me. It made his hand look like a mountain, and I was protected in the cleft of the rock. The enemy couldn't reach me; I was secure and protected in His hand. That's what prayer does for me.

I am sure you know God is no respecter of person, he has all of us in his hands. When I was little, we sang the song, "He's got the whole world, in his hands." He really does!

"Behold, I have graven thee upon the palms of *my* hands; thy walls are continually before me."
– Isaiah 49:16

We are in the palm of God's hand, so do not fear change.

"Prayer is that key that unlocks the doors."

## Your notes on the importance of prayer:

_____

_____

_____

_____

_____

_____

_____

_____

_____

_____

_____

_____

_____

_____

_____

_____

_____

_____

_____

_____

_____

_____

# References

Unless otherwise noted, scripture quotations are taken from the Holy Bible, King James Version.

"Fear." Poem written by Julia Terry-Myles. *Writings From My Sistahs!!!* Published Feb. 13, 2012

Joyce Meyer Ministries – Blog
https://www.joycemeyer.org/everydayanswers/ea-teachings/three-steps-to-emotional-healing-that-lasts

# Reflections

_____

_____

_____

_____

_____

_____

_____

_____

_____

_____

_____

_____

_____

_____

_____

_____

_____

_____

_____

_____

_____

_____

# Reflections

_____

_____

_____

_____

_____

_____

_____

_____

_____

_____

_____

_____

_____

_____

_____

_____

_____

_____

_____

_____

# Reflections

_____

_____

_____

_____

_____

_____

_____

_____

_____

_____

_____

_____

_____

_____

_____

_____

_____

_____

_____

_____

# Reflections

_____

_____

_____

_____

_____

_____

_____

_____

_____

_____

_____

_____

_____

_____

_____

_____

_____

_____

_____

_____

# Reflections

_____

_____

_____

_____

_____

_____

_____

_____

_____

_____

_____

_____

_____

_____

_____

_____

_____

_____

_____

_____

_____

# Reflections

_____

_____

_____

_____

_____

_____

_____

_____

_____

_____

_____

_____

_____

_____

_____

_____

_____

_____

_____

_____

# Reflections

_____

_____

_____

_____

_____

_____

_____

_____

_____

_____

_____

_____

_____

_____

_____

_____

_____

_____

_____

_____

_____

# Reflections

_____

_____

_____

_____

_____

_____

_____

_____

_____

_____

_____

_____

_____

_____

_____

_____

_____

_____

_____

_____

# Reflections

_____

_____

_____

_____

_____

_____

_____

_____

_____

_____

_____

_____

_____

_____

_____

_____

_____

_____

_____

_____

_____

# Reflections

_____

_____

_____

_____

_____

_____

_____

_____

_____

_____

_____

_____

_____

_____

_____

_____

_____

_____

_____

_____

_____

_____

# Reflections

_____

_____

_____

_____

_____

_____

_____

_____

_____

_____

_____

_____

_____

_____

_____

_____

_____

_____

# Reflections

# Reflections

_____

_____

_____

_____

_____

_____

_____

_____

_____

_____

_____

_____

_____

_____

_____

_____

_____

_____

_____

_____

# Reflections

_____

_____

_____

_____

_____

_____

_____

_____

_____

_____

_____

_____

_____

_____

_____

_____

_____

_____

_____

# Reflections

_____

_____

_____

_____

_____

_____

_____

_____

_____

_____

_____

_____

_____

_____

_____

_____

_____

_____

_____

_____

_____

# Reflections

_____

_____

_____

_____

_____

_____

_____

_____

_____

_____

_____

_____

_____

_____

_____

_____

_____

_____

_____

_____

# Reflections

_____

_____

_____

_____

_____

_____

_____

_____

_____

_____

_____

_____

_____

_____

_____

_____

_____

_____

_____

_____

_____

_____

# Reflections

_____

_____

_____

_____

_____

_____

_____

_____

_____

_____

_____

_____

_____

_____

_____

_____

_____

_____

_____

_____

# Reflections

# Reflections